CONTENTS

KW-115-240

	PAGE
X-Men: The Last Stand	**4 – 55**
People and places	4
Prologue: Twenty years ago ...	6
Chapter 1: A voice from the past	9
Chapter 2: The cure	13
Chapter 3: An amazing gift	18
Chapter 4: The Phoenix	22
Chapter 5: First blood	28
Chapter 6: A time of darkness	33
Chapter 7: War begins	38
Chapter 8: X-Men together	43
Chapter 9: A brave fight	47
Chapter 10: Logan's choice	51
Fact Files	**56 – 61**
The film	56
Marvel and the X-Men comics	58
San Francisco	60
Self-Study Activities	**62 – 64**

THE X-MEN

The X-Men are a team of mutants. Mutants are people with very special powers.

PROFESSOR CHARLES XAVIER

He has a special school for mutants. He can read and control people's minds.

SCOTT SUMMERS/ CYCLOPS

The strong beam from his eyes can cut through anything.

STORM

She can control the weather. She can make lightning, fog, strong winds …

LOGAN

He has the power to heal his body. He has metal claws in his hands and metal throughout his body.

ROGUE

She can take the power of other mutants for a short time. If she touches anyone for too long, her power can kill.

BOBBY DRAKE / ICEMAN

He has the power to make ice and freeze anything.

KITTY PRYDE

She can pass through anything and anything can pass through her.

COLOSSUS

He has the power to change his body into hard metal.

MAGNETO'S MUTANTS

MAGNETO / ERIC LENSHERR
He can move anything metal with his mind.

MYSTIQUE
This blue mutant can change shape to look like anyone and anything.

JUGGERNAUT
When he starts running *nothing* can stop this huge, strong mutant.

CALLISTO
She can move at super-speed. She can also 'feel' other mutants and their powers.

PYRO
He has power over fire. He used to go to Professor Xavier's school for mutants.

OTHER MUTANTS
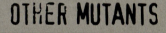

HANK MCCOY / BEAST
His body is covered by thick blue hair. He is fast and very strong.

PLACES

Westchester, New York: Charles Xavier's school for mutants is here.
Washington, DC: This city is the centre of the United States government. The President of the US lives and works here.
Alkali Lake: This is in Canada. The X-Men believe that Jean Grey died here.
San Francisco: This is a city on the south-west coast of the USA.
Alcatraz: This is an island off the coast of San Francisco.

JEAN GREY
She can move things with her mind and read other people's minds. The X-Men think that she died in Alkali Lake.

PROLOGUE TWENTY YEARS AGO ...

'We're not going to meet every one of them, are we?' Eric Lensherr asked as he looked around the quiet street.

'No. This one is special,' replied Charles Xavier, walking towards one of the houses.

The two men were good friends. Twenty years later they would be terrible enemies.

Soon they were sitting in the living room while Mr and Mrs Grey read the information about Xavier's School for Gifted Youngsters.

'It looks wonderful. It's a beautiful place,' said Mrs Grey. 'What do you think, John?'

Her husband looked worried. 'It looks great. But what about Jean? What about her . . . illness?'

'You think your daughter is sick?' Lensherr said angrily.

'Eric, please,' said Xavier. He didn't want anything to go wrong. He turned to Jean's parents. 'We want to help children like your daughter. Maybe we should talk to her alone.'

'Of course,' Mrs Grey replied, and she called upstairs. 'Jean? Can you come down, dear?' Xavier could hear something in the mother's voice – was it fear?

A few moments later the young girl appeared. She was about thirteen years old with beautiful red hair.

'We'll leave you then,' said Mrs Grey.

Jean didn't speak, but she gave the two men a long, cold look.

'That's very rude . . .' Xavier began. Then he used his power to speak silently inside Jean's mind. 'It's rude, you know, to read other people's thoughts.'

Jean looked suddenly surprised.

'Did you think that you were the only one like you?' said Lensherr.

'We are mutants*, Jean,' explained Xavier. 'We are like you.'

A smile appeared on the girl's face. 'Really? I don't think so.'

Slowly both men turned and looked out of the window. Every car on the street was in the air, metres above the ground!

Now Lensherr understood – this girl *was* special. 'I *like* this one,' he said with a smile.

But Xavier was very serious. 'You have more power than you can imagine,' he told Jean. 'The question is – will you control that power, or will it control you?'

Ten years later, in another part of the country, Warren Worthington Senior** was getting very worried.

'Son, is everything OK in there?' He knocked again on the bathroom door.

'Yes!' the boy replied, but he sounded afraid.

'Open this door now!' cried the father.

'One second!' Inside the bathroom, twelve-year-old Warren Worthington Junior tried to put away the tools that he was using. But he wasn't quick enough. His father

---

* A mutant is a person with special powers.
** When a father and son have the same name, the father is called 'Senior' and the son is called 'Junior'.

pushed the door open. He saw his son's pale face and the blood on the floor, and then he saw the things that were growing on his son's back. The boy had tried to cut them off, but Worthington could see what they were – the beginnings of wings.

'Not you . . . ' he said. Worthington Senior was a rich man; he usually got everything that he wanted. Now his worst nightmare had come true – his own son was a mutant!

Over the next ten years Worthington Senior found the best scientists in the world. He gave them the best equipment and laboratories.

Now he watched scientist Dr. Kavita Rao work in his laboratories on Alcatraz Island.

Years ago the island had been a prison, but now it was the home of Worthington's centre for the study of mutants.

Dr. Rao was working on a young boy called Leech. The boy was about twelve years old and he had big blue eyes and a shaved head. He was a mutant with a very special power. Maybe this boy was the answer to the problem Worthington had thought about for so long . . .

CHAPTER 1 A VOICE FROM THE PAST

A city at night. Many of the buildings were destroyed. The air was full of smoke and the sound of explosions. But one man walked through this terrible place looking calm. It was Logan, one of the X-Men and one of the most dangerous mutants in the world. In a fight he could use the long metal claws in his hands – claws that could cut through anyone or anything.

Storm used her weather power to fly ahead of the X-Men and lead them through the city. Suddenly a strong light shone down and there was an explosion. Pieces of metal flew towards Rogue, but Colossus moved quickly. Using his power, he made his whole body metal. Then he reached out and held Rogue. She was able to take the power of any mutant she touched. Immediately, she became metal, too.

Logan wasn't so lucky – the flying metal hit him right in the face. But he didn't care – his body had the power to heal itself immediately.

Two more young X-Men were following behind them – Bobby Drake and Kitty Pryde. Suddenly, a piece of metal shot towards the two teenage mutants. Quickly Bobby turned and shot ice at the metal and it fell to the ground. But another piece of metal was right behind the first. Kitty cried out and held Bobby close. Her power allowed things to go straight through her body. And when she touched another mutant, they could use her power, too. The piece of metal went straight through their bodies without any pain.

Quickly Bobby turned and used his power. He held up his hand and shot ice at the metal. It fell straight to the ground.

Storm found Logan resting against a car. 'They're killing us out here,' she said.

'These kids aren't ready yet,' Logan replied.

Suddenly, Storm jumped forward and pushed him to one side. Moments later a huge metal foot crashed down and destroyed the car. The enemy had seen them. Now lights were shining down and something was moving towards them. Something really big.

'Stay together!' Storm shouted to the others. 'We move as a *team*.'

'Good luck with that,' said Logan. He was getting tired of all this. SNIKT! His metal claws were out and ready. 'Throw me,' he said to Colossus.

'Logan, don't do it . . .' began Storm, but Colossus had already turned his body to metal. He picked Logan up easily and threw him towards the enemy in the dark.

The X-Men heard the sound of Logan's claws. Then moments later something fell to the ground – a huge metal head. The enemy was destroyed!

A moment later the city around them disappeared. The walls of the Danger Room were all the X-Men could see now. Professor Xavier had built this place for the X-Men to train in. The room was in his school in Westchester, but it could look like anywhere in the world.

'Hey, Colossus,' said Logan. 'Nice throw!'

As they left the Danger Room, Storm spoke angrily to Logan. 'What *was* that? I was trying to teach them something.'

'Well, I taught them something,' Logan joked, but Storm wasn't smiling. She wanted him to work as part of the team.

Logan didn't want to argue with her. She could talk to their leader, Scott, if she had a problem.

Scott Summers – Cyclops – had been the leader of the X-Men for many years. Now he was a different man. He hadn't slept or shaved for days. He just sat on the edge of his bed and almost cried. A terrible picture was always in his mind – a woman under the cold waters of Alkali Lake in Canada. It was Jean Grey, the love of his life. She had died in Alkali Lake to save the other X-Men.

And then he heard a whisper in his mind. It was Jean. She was saying his name, 'Scott!' Was he going crazy? Was Jean still alive? Scott knew one thing – he *had* to find out. He picked up his bag and left the room.

In another part of the school, Bobby Drake was running after his girlfriend, Rogue.

'What's wrong?' he asked.

'Nothing . . . except that I can't touch my boyfriend without killing him,' said Rogue.

'That's not fair,' said Bobby. 'Have I ever said anything?'

'You're a guy, Bobby. I know you want more . . .' she said and she walked away. Bobby just stood and watched her go.

Scott was on his way out of the school when Logan stopped him.

'They were looking for you in the Danger Room,' said Logan.

'What do you care?' said Scott. He and Logan had never liked each other.

'I had to take your place.'

'I didn't ask you to,' said Scott.

'No, the Professor did.'

'So?'

Logan fought to control himself. 'I know how you feel.'

'Don't,' said Scott.

'When Jean died . . .'

'I said don't!'

Jean had been Scott's girlfriend. But Logan had loved her, too.

Logan stepped closer and said, 'Maybe it's time to move on.'

'Not everybody heals as fast as you,' said Scott.

With these words, Scott pushed past Logan and out of the school. Moments later he was on his motorbike on his way to Alkali Lake.

CHAPTER 2 THE CURE

Hank McCoy was in his office in Washington, DC. He was hanging upside down and reading a science magazine.

Hank McCoy was a top politician in the United States government. He was also a mutant – a mutant covered in thick blue hair so he looked like a big animal. Once he had been one of Charles Xavier's X-Men. His name back then was Beast* and the name still suited him.

'The meeting's begun, sir,' said a government assistant.

'Thank you,' McCoy replied and jumped quickly to the floor.

Minutes later he entered the meeting room where the President and several members of his team were sitting around a large table. Hank sat down in the empty seat next to the President.

'Our people were following Magneto's movements,' the President said.

Politician Bolivar Trask gave more information: 'He was seen in Lisbon, Geneva, Montreal . . . We lost him when he crossed into the USA. But we did catch somebody else . . .'

He pointed to a screen which showed a small prison cell. The prisoner had blue skin and yellow eyes. It was the mutant Mystique.

'We caught her breaking into the FDA**,' explained Trask.

The politicians watched a screen as a government officer sat down opposite Mystique in the cell.

'Raven,' he began.

* A beast is any big wild animal.
** The FDA is the US government department for food and medicines.

Mystique's yellow eyes burned with hate. 'I don't answer to my human name.'

'It's the name that your family gave you,' said the officer. 'Don't you care about your family?'

'My family tried to kill me,' said Mystique angrily.

'So now *he's* your family?' The man was talking about Magneto. 'Where is he?'

'I don't know who you're talking about,' she replied. Then suddenly she changed so that she looked exactly like the officer. It was like looking into a mirror. Then she moved closer and whispered, 'I'll tell you where he is . . .'

The man moved closer, ready to hear more. POW! Mystique jumped up and hit him in the face with her head.

Immediately, guards ran into the room.

The President, Trask and McCoy watched the screen as the guards pulled Mystique off.

'Putting Mystique in prison will of course make Magneto even more angry and dangerous,' said McCoy. 'But it does give us more power when we talk to his people.'

The President looked surprised. 'You expect me to *talk* to these people?'

'Isn't that why you asked me to this meeting?' asked McCoy.

The President shook his head and passed a report to the mutant. 'This is. This is what Mystique stole from the FDA.'

McCoy started to look at the report. Immediately he saw the photo of a young boy about twelve years old with big blue eyes and a shaved head. Below the photo he read the name LEECH and the words CURE FOR MUTANTS. He looked up slowly with fear in his eyes. 'Does this "cure" work?'

'We think so,' answered the President.

'This will change everything for mutants everywhere.'

'Yes,' agreed the President. 'That's why we need you, Hank.'

'Power can be a very dangerous thing,' Professor Xavier was telling the class of teenage mutants. 'We must all learn this lesson because we are mutants. When is it OK to use our powers? When do they give us too much control over others? The line between the two is sometimes impossible to see.'

'Then how do we know when we've crossed it?' asked Kitty Pryde.

'How do we decide what is right and what is wrong?' Xavier began. Then he stopped, suddenly silent. Outside, the sky was dark with storm clouds.

'We'll continue this lesson tomorrow,' he told the class.

'The weather report said sunny skies,' said Xavier. He had come to the front of the school where Storm was standing. She was the reason for the dark clouds above.

'Oh . . . I'm sorry,' she said. Her eyes turned white as she used her power over the weather. Moments later the bright, sunny day was back.

'I don't need to read minds to see that something is wrong,' continued Xavier as they went together into the school.

'Magneto isn't a problem for us now,' said Storm. 'We have a mutant politician in the government. We have a President who understands us. Why are we still hiding?'

'We are *not* hiding,' Xavier replied. 'We still have enemies out there and I have to protect my students.'

Storm watched the students going to their next class. 'Yes, but we can't be students forever.'

'Storm, I haven't thought of you as my student for many years. In fact . . .' He stopped at the door to his office. 'I have started to think that you might take my place one day.'

A look of surprise appeared on Storm's face. 'But Scott . . .'

'Scott's a changed man,' said Xavier. 'Jean's death has been so hard for him.'

Storm didn't know what to say.

'Things *are* better for us out there,' continued Xavier. 'But you of all people should know how fast the weather can change.'

'There's something you're not telling us,' Storm said. She could see it in his eyes.

When they went into Xavier's office, they found an old friend waiting there – Hank McCoy. Storm ran to Beast and hugged him.

'I have some news,' said McCoy. 'Mystique was caught last week. We don't have . . .'

'Who's the big ball of hair?' asked a voice suddenly from the door. It was Logan.

'I'm Hank McCoy.'

'Right. Nice suit,' Logan replied as he entered the room.

Storm was still thinking about Mystique. 'Magneto isn't going to be happy about this,' she said.

'Magneto isn't our biggest problem,' said McCoy. 'A company has made a new medicine for mutants. They're calling it a "cure".'

These words hung for a moment in the air, and then . . .

'That's crazy!' cried Storm. 'You can't *cure* being a mutant!'

'Storm,' said Xavier, pointing to a TV screen. 'They're announcing it right now.'

CHAPTER 3 AN AMAZING GIFT

Warren Worthington Senior stood outside his Alcatraz laboratories. Dr Rao was behind him, and reporters and TV cameras were all around them.

'Mutants are people just like us. They are ill. Today I am proud to announce the answer to the mutant problem.' He held up a small bottle. 'Finally, we have . . . a cure!'

Everyone in Xavier's office was silent after they heard this announcement. Their world was never going to be the same again.

'Who would want this cure?' asked Storm angrily. 'Just to be accepted by others?'

'It isn't so easy for all of us to be accepted,' said McCoy looking down at his blue hairy hands.

'Maybe this was the government's idea,' said Logan.

'The government had *nothing* to do with this,' said McCoy.

'I've heard that before,' said Logan.

Suddenly an excited voice spoke from the door. 'Is it true? They can cure us?' It was Rogue.

'Yes, Rogue,' said Xavier. 'It appears to be true.'

'No, Professor', said Storm angrily. 'They can't cure us. Because there's nothing wrong with you. Or with any of us!'

It was night in the city, and lots of people were going into an old church. A sign outside the door said: MUTANT ACTION MEETING. At the bottom of the sign it said: NO HUMANS ALLOWED.

Inside, lots of mutants were listening to a man at the front of the church. 'We just have to speak to the right people,' he was saying. 'We have to talk to the government about this.'

'The government is trying to kill us!' shouted a young mutant angrily. He was standing with a group of other young mutants. None of them wanted a cure – they were proud to be mutants.

'We're free to choose the cure or not,' said the man at the front. 'Nobody is talking about killing mutants.'

'No one *ever* talks about it,' shouted a deep voice from the back of the church. 'They just do it!'

Everybody turned to see Magneto. A young man was with him – Pyro. He had been a student at Xavier's school before he joined Magneto.

'And then one night they come for you,' continued Magneto. 'That's when you realise – while you were having meetings, they were starting to kill.'

The church was silent. Everyone looked at Magneto. 'Believe me,' he continued. 'They will make us take this cure. The only question is: who will you stand with? The humans . . . or us?'

As Magneto left the church, the group of angry young mutants stopped him.

'That's big talk for an old man,' said one of them.

Pyro pushed the young mutant back. 'Do you know who you're talking to?'

'Do *you*?' replied the young man, whose mutant name was Quill. Immediately, long black needles appeared from every part of his body.

Magneto smiled at the young mutants – they were his kind of people. He turned to a young woman from the group called Callisto. 'And what can *you* do?'

Suddenly, she moved so fast that he couldn't really see her. One moment she was a few metres away. The next moment she was right in front of him.

'I can do that and more,' she said and turned to Pyro. 'I know that you can control fire . . . And you can control metal,' she said to Magneto. 'I know that there are eighty-seven mutants in here. You two are the only ones who are more powerful than class three.'

Magneto smiled. 'So you can feel other mutants and their powers. Could you find one for me?' He was thinking of Mystique.

Dr Rao led Hank McCoy through the Worthington Laboratories building on Alcatraz.

'How long will you keep the boy here?' McCoy asked. He was there to find out more about the cure.

'A little longer,' Rao answered. 'Soon we'll be able to make the cure without him.'

They stepped into a bright white room with toys and

books on the floor. A twelve-year-old boy sat playing a video game.

'I'd like you to meet someone,' said Dr Rao.

Leech looked up nervously.

'Hello there. My name is Hank McCoy.' He held out his hand. But as it came closer to Leech, something happened – the blue hair and colour disappeared. For the first time in his life, McCoy had a normal, human hand.

'I'm sorry,' said Leech.

It was hard for McCoy to find the words. 'It's . . . OK.'

As McCoy moved his hand away from Leech, the blue hair and colour came back.

'You have an amazing gift,' he said to the boy.

CHAPTER 4 THE PHOENIX

Scott looked out at the shining waters of Alkali Lake. He put a hand to his head as he heard Jean's voice again: 'Scott . . . Scott!'

He shook his head, trying to escape from the voice. 'STOP!' he cried and pulled off his glasses. Immediately a red beam shot out from his eyes into the water. Scott's mutant name was Cyclops and his eyes fired a powerful beam. This beam could cut through anything and only his special glasses could stop it.

He shut his eyes and fell to his knees. His face was wet with tears.

Suddenly the waters of the lake started to move. Then the waters shot up, knocking Scott back. He put his glasses back on and looked up into a bright light. Someone was inside the light, coming closer. 'Jean . . .?' he said.

It was true – Jean was in front of him, alive!

'Scott,' she whispered.

His tears of pain became tears of happiness.

'How . . .?'

Jean looked down at her body, feeling its power. 'I don't know.'

Scott took her in his arms and hugged her.

'I want to see your eyes,' she said. 'Take your glasses off.'

Scott pulled away from her. He could never take his glasses off. Without them, he couldn't control the beam.

'I can control it,' said Jean, slowly taking off his glasses. At first, he was afraid to open his eyes.

'Open them,' whispered Jean. 'You can't hurt me.'

Slowly Scott opened his eyes and . . . nothing happened. No beam came out. For the first time in his life, he looked into the eyes of the love of his life. The two kissed.

But something was wrong. Jean's eyes looked very strange. Suddenly Scott's skin started to shiver. Jean had so much power now – too much power. And then there was an explosion of light. Scott's eyes opened wide with fear. The last thing that he saw was this bright, white light. And then nothing.

Back at the school in Westchester, Professor Xavier screamed in pain. Students all around the school could hear the scream in their minds. They held their heads in pain, too.

Logan and Storm both ran to Xavier's office.

'Are you OK?' asked Logan.

Xavier's face was pale. 'Go to Alkali Lake,' he told them. 'Now!'

Alkali Lake had bad memories for Storm and for Logan. Jean had died there to save them, but they were X-Men and they had a job to do. They ran to the X-Jet, the team's plane. Minutes later, they were flying north to Canada.

When Storm and Logan arrived at the lake, the place was covered with thick fog.

'I can help with that,' said Storm. Her eyes went white and the fog soon disappeared.

But something still wasn't right and they knew it. As they searched the area, Logan found something just sitting in the air – Scott's glasses. He picked them out of the air, not understanding. If Scott's glasses were here, where was Scott?

Then he heard Storm shout from further down the beach: 'Logan!'

He ran over to her and his eyes opened in surprise. He couldn't believe it – Jean was lying there on the beach!

'She's alive,' said Storm.

'Jean was the only class five mutant I've ever met,' Xavier said to Logan back at the school in Westchester. 'Her powers were almost without end.'

He looked down at Jean, who was sleeping deeply.

'Jean's powers came from a deep part of her mind. Her powers were too dangerous and so I built several barriers in her mind. I wanted to keep Jean's full powers away from her conscious mind. But slowly she started to have two personalities. There was the conscious Jean with her powers always in control. But deep down there was another personality – an angry beast that cared only for itself. We called this personality the Phoenix*.'

'Did Jean know all this?' asked Logan.

'I don't know,' answered Xavier. 'And I don't know if the woman in front of us now is Jean . . . or the Phoenix. But I'm trying to build those barriers in her mind again and control the beast.'

'What have you done to her?' Logan cried angrily. 'You're talking about a person's mind!'

'She *has* to be controlled. You have no idea what she could do.'

'I didn't know what *you* could do,' answered Logan sharply.

'I had a terrible choice to make,' Xavier said as he moved towards the door.

'Jean didn't have a choice at all,' replied Logan.

'I don't have to explain myself to you,' said the Professor and he left the room.

Warren Worthington Senior, was looking out of the window of his offices in the centre of San Francisco. A group of mutants stood outside shouting angrily about the cure. A bigger group of people were standing in line hoping to receive it. But Worthington knew who should be the first to get the cure.

His son Warren was led into the room. He looked nervous to be there.

'Hello, Warren,' said Dr Rao.

* A phoenix is a bird in stories from long ago. After it dies in a fire, the phoenix is born again.

'I'm proud of you, son, for doing this,' said Worthington Senior. 'Are you ready?'

'Yes,' Warren said weakly as he took off his coat and shirt. There was something on his back – he had tied it up with straps so that it couldn't move.

Dr Rao took out the needle and brought it towards Warren.

'Dad, can we just talk about this?'

'We already talked about it, son.'

'Wait,' said Warren. 'I . . . I can't do this.'

The doctor's assistants held him down, but Warren started to fight back. As he did this, the straps on his back broke. Two huge, white wings appeared. Everyone in the room stopped and looked at the amazing wings.

At last, his father found words. 'Warren, it's what we all want.'

'No!' shouted Warren. 'It's what *you* want!'

He saw the guards at the door and so he ran to the windows.

'Warren, no!' shouted his father. But Warren jumped straight through the glass.

The people outside looked up and saw an amazing sight – a man with wings flying over their heads!

Warren flew high over the buildings, over the island of Alcatraz, and out of the city.

The young boy Leech watched this beautiful sight from a window in Worthington's laboratories on Alcatraz. Maybe one day soon he would also be free?

CHAPTER 5 FIRST BLOOD

'Let me out,' said the man in the metal cell. 'I'm the President of the United States!'

'Mr President?' said the prison guard. 'Shut up!'

When the guard looked at the cell again, the President wasn't there. Now a little girl was looking at him. 'I'll be a good girl. Please let me go!'

When the guard gave no answer, the girl smiled and whispered, 'I'm going to kill you when I get out of here.'

The prisoner wasn't really the President or a little girl – it was the mutant Mystique. And the metal cell was inside a moving prison truck. They were moving Mystique and several other dangerous mutants around the country – they didn't want Magneto to find them.

But it was already too late. With Callisto's help Magneto had found the prison truck. And now he stood in the middle of the empty road and waited for it to arrive.

Using his power over metal, he destroyed the two police cars in front of the truck. Then he destroyed the two cars behind. Then he lifted up the back of the truck and it crashed down onto the road. Inside, everyone fell forward. One guard fell unconscious. The other guard started to get up, but suddenly blue feet came out from Mystique's cell and closed around his neck.

'I told you that I'd kill you,' she said. Then she took the prison keys with her feet.

Suddenly the back doors of the truck flew off and Magneto was standing there. Pyro and Callisto followed him into the truck.

'About time,' said Mystique.

'I've been busy,' answered Magneto with a little smile. 'Did you find what you were looking for?'

'They're using a mutant child to make the cure. He's at Worthington Laboratories on Alcatraz.'

Magneto thought about this for a moment then turned to the prison cells. 'Who do we have here?' he asked.

Pyro read out the names from the guards' notes. 'This is James Madrox.'

'He robbed several banks,' explained Mystique. 'All at the same time.'

A man walked out of the open cell. Then another man who looked exactly the same as the first. Then another, and another, and another.

'His mutant name is Multiple Man,' said Pyro. 'He can make copies of himself.'

Magneto smiled. 'I could use a man like you.'

'I'm in,' Madrox replied.

The mutant in the next cell was huge. His arms and legs and even his head were held down with strong metal.

'He's called Cain Marko,' Pyro read from the notes. 'Listen: "The prisoner must be kept still at all times. If he reaches enough speed, *nothing* can stop him."'

Magneto looked at the huge mutant. 'What do they call you?'

'Juggernaut!'

'Join us!' said Magneto.

As the mutants were about to escape from the truck, one of the guards became conscious again. Quickly, he put a special dart into his gun and pointed it at Magneto. But Mystique saw him and jumped in front of Magneto. The gun's dart hit her instead of Magneto.

The guard tried to shoot a second time, but Magneto pulled the gun from the guard's hand with his mind. Then Pyro shot fire at him.

It was all too late for Mystique. She lay on the floor in terrible pain. Her body was changing. When she looked up, she had lost her blue colour. Her eyes weren't yellow now. She was a normal human. For a moment Magneto looked at her with pity. 'You saved me,' he said. But then he turned and walked away.

'Eric!' Mystique called to him.

'I'm sorry. You're not one of us now,' he said coldly as he left the truck with the other mutants. 'It's a pity. She was so beautiful,' he said to them.

Logan was standing by Jean's side when suddenly she opened her eyes and held onto his arm.

'Logan,' she said smiling.

'Welcome back,' he replied, but he already felt there was something different about her.

'Are you OK?' he asked.

'Yeah, more than OK.'

Logan looked at her beautiful face.

Then Jean pulled Logan close and kissed him. For several moments they kissed, but Logan started to feel very strange.

'Wait,' he said. 'Jean, this . . . isn't you. Perhaps you should rest. The Professor said that you might be different.'

Jean suddenly looked very angry.

'Jean . . . where's Scott?' asked Logan.

Something in her changed. She looked around the room, suddenly unsure of where she was. 'I'm sorry . . . Where am I?'

'Back in the school. Jean, you need to tell me what happened to Scott.'

Jean's eyes filled with tears as she thought of Scott. 'Oh no!' she said as she remembered what happened at Alkali Lake. Things around the room started to move and shake. Jean whispered, 'Kill me, Logan. Please. Before I kill someone else. KILL ME!'

'No! We can help you. The Professor can help . . .'

'I don't *want* to be helped,' said Jean, suddenly angry again. With the power of her mind, she picked Logan up and threw him against the wall. He could do nothing to stop her.

She walked out of the room, leaving Logan unconscious on the floor.

Storm and Xavier found Logan several hours later as he started to wake up.

'What happened?' asked Storm.

'What have you done?' asked the Professor.

Logan sat up slowly. 'It's Jean . . . I think she killed Scott.'

'What?' said Storm. 'It's not possible.'

'I told you what she can do,' said Xavier. He closed his eyes and tried to find Jean with his mind. 'She's left the school,' he said, 'but she's stopping me from reading her thoughts. She's so strong.' He stopped for a moment then said, 'I think I know where she's going. I hope we're not too late.'

In a dark room under ground, Magneto held up the gun that had shot Mystique. 'I told you that they would hit us first,' he said to his mutants. 'The time has come to prepare for war.'

As they were about to leave, Callisto came down the stairs into the room. 'I felt something today,' she said to Magneto. 'It was a mutant, class five. Stronger than you.'

He knew who Callisto was talking about. 'Where is she?' Magneto asked.

CHAPTER 6 A TIME OF DARKNESS

Professor Xavier was back outside Jean's old house, but this time he was with Storm and Logan. The street hadn't changed much in the last twenty years.

'Wait for me here. I need to see Jean alone,' he told the two X-Men.

And then he heard his old friend's voice. 'You were right, Charles. This one is special,' said Magneto.

'What are you doing here?' asked Logan.

'The same as the Professor – visiting an old friend.'

'I don't want any trouble,' said Xavier.

'Neither do I,' said Magneto. 'Let's go inside.'

Xavier and Magneto went towards the house together. As he passed his mutants, Magneto said to Juggernaut, 'Stay here and make sure no one gets inside.'

Everything was quiet inside the house, but it wasn't calm. Xavier could see things all around the house shaking and moving. He could feel the power in this place.

Jean was sitting in the living room, pale and alone.

'I knew you would come,' she said quietly.

'I've come to bring you home,' Xavier replied.

'I have no home.'

'Yes, you do. You have a home and a family.'

Magneto stepped forward. 'He thinks your power is too great for you to control.'

'So you want to control me?' she said to Xavier.

'No, I want to help you,' he said.

'What's wrong with me?'

'Nothing at all!' said Magneto.

'Eric, stop!' said Xavier.

'No, Charles, you've always held her back.'

'It was only to help you, Jean.'

But Jean looked really angry. A lamp flew across the room and crashed against the wall. More and more things were moving now – tables, chairs, books . . . But Xavier's eyes did not leave Jean. 'Look at me, Jean. I can help you.'

'You want to give her the cure!' cried Magneto.

Xavier's eyes closed as he tried to get inside Jean's mind.

'No, stop it!' she shouted. A wave of power suddenly broke all the windows and sent Magneto flying out of the room.

The mutants waiting in the street outside heard the noise – they knew that something was very wrong.

'That's it. I'm going in,' said Logan. SNIKT! SNIKT! Logan's claws shot out from his hands and he ran straight towards Juggernaut. But Juggernaut was bigger and stronger and he threw Logan into the air. When Logan crashed down on the ground, Juggernaut just picked him up and threw him through a window into Jean's house.

Using her weather power, Storm rose up into the air. Then, turning her body around and around, she flew very fast towards Magneto's mutants. The strong wind knocked Quill and a young mutant called Arclight to one side. Then she shot lightning at Callisto and knocked her into the house. Using her super-speed, Callisto moved quickly and hit Storm hard in the face.

Juggernaut had followed Logan into the house. Now he picked Logan up and threw him up into the air and through to the floor above.

In the living room Jean and Xavier were locked in a war of minds.

'Jean, let me in!' cried Xavier.

Their faces shivered and Xavier's body slowly rose up out of his chair. Little pieces of Xavier's skin and clothes started to fly from his body.

Magneto could see what was happening and cried out, 'No, Jean!'

But Jean's power was growing stronger every second and at that moment the whole house rose up into the air!

Storm and Logan had managed to escape their attackers. They tried to reach the Professor, but Jean's power was pulling them back. Jean lifted her arms and a strong golden light shone around her. For several moments everything slowed right down and the Professor said to Jean, 'Don't let your power control you.' Then he turned his head towards Logan. He gave a little smile, and then his body exploded into a million pieces.

Magneto got up and walked through the broken walls

of the house to Jean. 'Come with me, my dear,' he said, and they left the house together.

Storm and Logan ran into the living room, but all they found was the Professor's empty chair. Logan fell to his knees and Storm put her arms around him. Both X-Men cried tears of pain and disbelief. Charles Xavier, the father of the X-Men, was dead.

Storm stood next to the grave of Professor Charles Xavier in the school gardens.

'We live in a time of darkness,' she said. 'But there are some people who fight the darkness. Charles Xavier was born into a world of hate and fear. He worked all his life to heal the world.'

Xavier's friends and students sat and listened in unhappy silence. He had been more than just a leader and teacher to them – he had been a friend.

'But Xavier's lessons live on with us, his students,' continued Storm. 'We must continue his dream of making this world a better place for mutants and humans.'

Storm's eyes found Logan. He was standing alone at the school entrance. He looked back at Storm and then turned away into the school.

Some time later, Rogue stood at the front door of the school, her suitcase in her hand.

'Where are you going, kid?' asked a deep voice.

She turned and saw Logan. She couldn't hide the suitcase – it was clear that she was leaving.

'You don't know what it's like,' she said. 'To be afraid of your powers . . . to be afraid to get close to anyone. I want to be able to *touch* people. A hug. A kiss . . .'

'I hope that you're not doing this for a boy,' said Logan.

Rogue looked away. She loved her boyfriend, Bobby. She hated the fact that she couldn't even hold hands with him.

'If you want to go, then go,' said Logan softly. 'Just be sure that it's what you want.'

Rogue looked up, surprised. 'Aren't you going to tell me to go back to my room?'

Logan put a hand on her shoulder. 'I'm not your father. I'm your friend. Take care, Rogue.'

She smiled. 'My real name is Marie.'

'Marie.'

Logan turned and left her alone. She waited for a moment, then opened the door and left the school.

CHAPTER 7 WAR BEGINS

Deep in the woods outside San Francisco hundreds of mutants had come to join Magneto. They were angry, afraid and ready to join the fight against the cure. Now they were waiting for Magneto's orders.

Jean Grey and Magneto looked down at them from higher up in the woods. Magneto lifted a gun into the air with his mind. It was the gun that had shot Mystique – the cure darts were still in it.

'I can control metal,' he said to Jean. 'But you can do anything.'

Immediately, Jean took control of the gun. She took the gun to pieces with her mind and moved the cure darts through the air.

Suddenly the darts were pointing straight at Magneto.

'Jean, enough!' cried Magneto. 'Enough!'

'You sound just like the Professor,' she said but she let the cure darts fall to the ground.

Magneto shook his head. 'Charles wanted to hold you back. I want you to be *what you are*. They want to give the cure to us all. If we want to be free, we must fight. And that fight begins now.'

The X-Men and Hank McCoy were in Xavier's office. Nobody knew what to say without the Professor.

Bobby Drake broke the silence.

'So what do we do next?' he asked.

'Professor Xavier started this school. Perhaps it should end with him,' said McCoy. 'We'll have to tell the students that they're going home.'

'Most of us don't have anywhere to go,' said Bobby. 'I can't believe that we're not going to fight for this place!'

At that moment a young man with blond hair appeared at the door. 'I'm sorry,' said Warren Worthington Junior. 'I know this is a bad time but I heard this was a safe place for mutants.'

'It was, son,' said McCoy.

But Storm had heard enough. 'And it still is. We'll find you a room.'

She walked behind Xavier's desk and looked at the others. This was her place now.

'Hank, tell all the students that the school will stay open.'

Bobby and Kitty smiled to hear this news, but Logan turned away, his face full of worry.

Bobby went to see Rogue. He wanted to tell her the good news – the school was going to stay open. He knocked on the door of her room and called out her name. There was no answer so he opened the door. Rogue wasn't there and all her things were gone.

Logan was standing beside Xavier's grave, deep in thought.

Suddenly, he heard something – a voice in his head. 'Logan! Logan!' it called. It was Jean's voice. In his mind he saw the trees and woods and the camp where Jean was. He fell to his knees and put a hand to his head to stop the pain.

Minutes later Logan was in his room putting his things into a bag.

Storm appeared at the door. 'Where are you going?'

'Where do you think?' Logan replied.

'She's gone, Logan. And she's not coming back.'

'You don't know that,' he replied.

'She killed the Professor.'

'That wasn't Jean. The real Jean's still in there.'

'Why can't you accept the truth?' asked Storm. 'Why can't you let her go?'

'Because . . . because . . .'

Storm understood. 'Because you love her.'

Logan didn't know what to say.

'She made her choice,' continued Storm. 'It's time to make ours. If you're with us, be with us.' With these words, she walked away, leaving Logan alone with his thoughts.

All around the country people stopped and watched their TV screens.

'Today there was an attack by my mutants on one of the Worthington buildings,' said Magneto looking straight into the camera. 'But this is just the start. Your cities will not be safe. *You* will not be safe. And to my brother mutants out there, I say join us, or stay out of our way!'

The President was watching this message in the White House. He turned to Bolivar Trask and said angrily, 'We cannot let him do this! I want soldiers in front of all the Worthington buildings. Make sure that they all have the plastic cure guns. And, Trask, you have to find Magneto and stop him – if he wants a war, we'll give him a war.'

Logan moved through the dark woods like an animal – fast, strong and silent. He knew this place. He had seen it in his mind when he heard Jean's voice. Now he was near Magneto's camp.

He had met several guards, but they couldn't beat Logan. He had cut them with his claws and now they were lying unconscious on the ground.

Logan moved through the trees towards the camp. He was surprised to see so many mutants. Magneto stood next to Jean and was speaking to the crowd below.

'They want to cure us,' Magneto said, 'but we are the cure! They have their cure guns, but we have the Phoenix!' He looked at Jean and then continued, 'We will go to

Alcatraz Island. We will take control of the cure and destroy it. Nothing will stop us!'

As Magneto said these final words, Jean walked away into the woods and Logan followed her. He called out to her and she turned around. She saw Logan and for a second she seemed to smile at him. He began to move closer, but suddenly his body was thrown against a tree. 'I can smell the metal in your body from a mile away,' said Magneto coldly.

Logan tried to move, but he wasn't able to. 'I didn't come to fight you,' he told Magneto. 'I came for her.' He looked towards Jean.

Magneto used his power to pull Logan closer. 'She is here because she *wants* to be.'

Logan spoke through the pain. 'I'm not leaving here without her.'

Magneto pulled him even closer and looked into his eyes. 'Yes, you are.'

Suddenly, Logan shot up into the air. He flew high above the trees and landed far away, half-dead and covered in blood.

CHAPTER 8 X-MEN TOGETHER

The White House, Washington, DC. The President and Bolivar Trask were watching a screen full of small bright lights. Each light was a mutant in Magneto's camp. In a few minutes, government soldiers were going to hit the camp. It had been very easy to find – Mystique, now fully human, had told them everything.

The government soldiers moved quickly through the woods. When the moment came, they all ran into the camp, ready to shoot at Magneto's mutants. But something was wrong – the camp was almost empty. Where were all the mutants? There were only five there now. Then four . . . then three . . . then two . . . then one!

It was the mutant called Multiple Man. He was the only person in the camp, but he had made copies of himself to trick the soldiers.

'You've got me,' he said, lifting up his hands.

Back at the White House, the President didn't understand. 'If Magneto's not there, then where is he?'

'Storm! Storm!' cried Logan when he arrived back at the school.

She ran to him and said, 'What are you doing back here?'

'Jean's with Magneto. We've got to go now. They're going to attack Alcatraz.'

'But there are soldiers on the island,' said Hank.

'Not enough to stop Magneto,' Logan replied.

Moments later the X-Men were in their special black suits. Beast was wearing his old suit from years ago – it was a bit tight for him now!

As they went to the X-Jet, Hank asked, 'How many people does Magneto have?'

'Hundreds!' Logan replied.

'But there are only six of us, Logan,' said Bobby.

'If we don't fight now, everything Scott and the Professor fought for will be lost,' Logan said. 'I'm not going to let that happen. We stand together – all of us – as X-Men.'

Bobby looked at the other two teenagers – Kitty and Colossus. They nodded and Bobby said, 'We're in. Let's go!'

As they got onto the X-Jet, Logan said to Storm, 'They're ready.'

'I know,' she said. 'But are *you* ready?'

Logan didn't know the answer to that. He didn't know what he was going to do when he saw Jean again.

As usual, there was a lot of traffic on San Francisco's Golden Gate Bridge. Suddenly the bridge began to shake and move. Many of the cars crashed and soon the traffic stopped completely.

A lot of people got out of their cars and tried to run off the bridge. But Magneto walked onto the bridge with some of his mutants. In the middle of the bridge, he lifted his hands in the air. Slowly one side of the metal bridge broke away and Magneto lifted it up into the air. Moments later the other side of the bridge broke free and also rose into the air. Magneto had lifted the Golden Gate Bridge! And now, under his control, it flew across the water towards Alcatraz.

When the bridge's position was right, Magneto simply let the bridge fall. In just a few minutes, Magneto had completely changed San Francisco – now the Golden Gate Bridge went from the city to Alcatraz!

Warren Worthington Senior watched from his laboratories with disbelief as Magneto led his mutants onto the island.

Callisto stood beside Magneto and Jean outside the Worthington laboratories. 'The boy is in the south-east corner of the building,' she said.

'Well then . . .' Magneto said looking at Pyro.

'Destroy the building!' Pyro shouted to all the mutants behind them.

The first wave of mutants attacked. Juggernaut wanted to join them, but Magneto stopped him. 'In chess, you never start with your best pieces.'

Suddenly, the soldiers guarding the building came forward and took out their guns. Magneto waved a hand, hoping to take the guns from the soldiers. When nothing happened he realized that the guns were plastic. 'They've learned!' he said in surprise.

The soldiers fired and cure darts flew through the air towards the first wave of mutants. At first the darts didn't seem to hurt the mutants. But then they started to shiver and shake and *change*. They cried out in pain as they lost their special powers and became human.

'That's why you don't start a chess game with your best pieces,' said Magneto to Juggernaut.

And now the soldiers were moving forward to attack again. This time they brought out bigger guns. These guns shot hundreds of darts into the air towards Magneto and his mutants. Immediately Magneto lifted three huge pieces of metal into the air and made a barrier. The darts hit the metal and fell to the ground.

Before the soldiers could fire again, Magneto turned to Arclight and said, 'Destroy those guns!'

Arclight's power allowed her to control sound waves. She hit her hands together and the sound waves shot out towards the soldiers. Immediately, their guns broke into little pieces. With no guns to protect them, the soldiers ran back to the building. Now they could do nothing to stop Magneto and his mutants.

CHAPTER 9 A BRAVE FIGHT

The X-Jet landed on top of the Worthington laboratories on Alcatraz Island. The X-Men jumped out one by one. Storm used her weather power to fly down to the ground. Beast jumped across the top of the Worthington building, then landed in front of it. Colossus turned his body metal and simply fell to the ground. Kitty held Bobby tight as they jumped. Because of her power, they passed right through the ground. Moments later, they came back up. Logan used his claws against the side of the building to slow his fall. Now the X-Men were ready. They stood in a line in front of the building and faced Magneto and all his mutants.

'Hold this line,' Logan told the others.

On the other side, Magneto looked at the X-Men angrily. 'Kill them all!' he shouted. Thirty or forty mutants ran forward to attack the X-Men.

All the X-Men fought bravely. Logan fought ten mutants back with his claws. Near him, Beast moved with amazing speed as he hit and kicked his attackers.

Storm rose up into the air but Callisto saw her. Callisto moved at super-speed to the top of the building. Then she jumped onto Storm and pulled her down to the ground.

Bobby shot a wall of ice at Magneto's mutants and stopped their attack.

Magneto turned to Juggernaut and said, 'Go inside, get the boy and kill him!'

Juggernaut smiled – at last he could join the fight. He put his head down, ran at the building and crashed easily through the walls.

'He's going to get Leech!' cried Beast to the X-Men.

'Not if I can get there first!' said Kitty.

The teenager ran at top speed after Juggernaut, passing straight through the outside walls. Soon she caught up with him and jumped onto his back. Using her power, she pulled him down into the floor. For a moment Juggernaut was stuck in the floor – he couldn't believe it! He cried out, 'Don't you know who I am? I'm the Juggernaut!'

Moments later, he broke out of the floor and ran after Kitty, crashing through wall after wall.

Kitty heard the terrible noise as Juggernaut came running behind her. She moved quickly to one side and hid. A moment later Juggernaut came crashing through and carried on running. He hadn't seen her.

In another part of the building, a group of Magneto's mutants had caught Warren Worthington Senior and Dr Rao.

Quill looked at Worthington with hate in his eyes. 'So you're the one who found the cure?'

'Yes,' answered Worthington, trying to be brave.

Arclight and another teenage mutant pulled Worthington towards the top of the building.

'Don't hurt him!' cried Dr Rao.

'Calm down. Everything's going to be OK,' said Quill as he put his arms around Dr Rao. But, suddenly, Quill shot out all the long black needles from his body. In a second Dr Rao was dead.

Kitty ran through the building, looking for Leech. Finally, she walked though a wall into a bright white room. The boy was hiding next to his bed. He looked up at her with frightened eyes.

'I'm here to help you,' Kitty told him. 'We've got to get you out of here.'

She held onto the boy and ran towards the wall . . . but they didn't go through it.

'What's happening?' Kitty wondered.

'Your powers won't work with me,' said Leech.

They could hear the sound of Juggernaut crashing through the walls – he wasn't far away.

'Stay close,' said Kitty.

Just then Juggernaut crashed into the room. He looked at Kitty and Leech and smiled.

Then, he put his head down and ran straight at them. At the last moment, Kitty held onto Leech and pulled him to the floor. Juggernaut's head missed them and he hit the wall at top speed. He fell unconscious to the floor. His powers didn't work because of Leech.

Kitty took Leech by the hand, and the two of them left

the room through the huge hole Juggernaut had made.

On the roof of the building, Magneto's mutants were holding Worthington over the edge.

'Please don't do this,' he said. 'I only want to help you people.'

'Do we look like we need your help?' said Quill.

And then they threw Worthington off the building.

As he fell into the darkness, he thought that this must be the end. But suddenly strong arms were holding him. He was safe! His son Warren had caught him in his arms. And now they were flying high above Alcatraz.

More and more mutants had come over the bridge to attack, but the X-Men never stopped fighting. Storm had finally beaten her enemy Callisto. She had thrown Callisto against a metal gate and then shot lightning at her. Now the teenager lay unconscious on the ground. Logan and Beast had fought off many attackers – they were as brave and strong as ten fighters.

Colossus and Bobby, too, had shown they were excellent fighters. And now there were many mutant bodies lying on the ground and the X-Men were winning.

But Magneto wasn't going to give up now. He turned to Pyro and said, 'Time to end this war!'

CHAPTER 10 LOGAN'S CHOICE

The X-Men looked up as a car flew high into the air. Suddenly the car was on fire. The burning car flew towards them. It was followed by another and then another. Magneto was sending cars from the bridge into the air and Pyro was setting them on fire.

The X-Men ran for cover behind the burning cars. Logan saw some of the cure darts lying on the ground. Storm and Beast saw them, too. A plan formed in Logan's mind.

'We work as a team,' he said. 'Bobby, can you stop your old friend?'

At one time Bobby and Pyro had been friends at Xavier's school. But they became enemies when Pyro left the school to join Magneto.

Bobby looked over at Pyro and said, 'Yes, I can stop him.'

Then Logan turned to Storm, 'We're going to need some cover.'

Storm's eyes went white as she started to make a thick fog.

The next car came flying out of the fog and Pyro set it on fire. Suddenly, ice killed the fire and the car dropped to the ground.

Bobby stepped forward and faced his old friend. Confident in his powers, Pyro lifted his arm and shot fire at Bobby.

The young X-Man acted immediately and shot ice at the fire. For a few moments the ice was pushing back the fire, but then the fire burned through the ice. Moments later Bobby was on his knees completely covered in fire.

'Same old Bobby,' said Pyro. 'Maybe you should go

back to school . . .'

This made Bobby very angry. He *had* to beat Pyro!
Suddenly his head and then his whole body turned to ice.
He held onto Pyro's arms and then hit Pyro with his head.
The cold, hard ice was like a rock and Pyro fell
unconscious to the ground.

'You should never have *left* the school!' Bobby said as he
walked away.

The whole of Alcatraz Island was covered in fog. The X-
Men could only just see Magneto and Jean now.

'Time to use your throwing arm,' Logan told Colossus.
He picked Logan up and threw him towards Magneto. It
was like in the Danger Room, but this time it was for real.

But because of the metal in Logan's body, Magneto
already knew he was coming.

Magneto lifted a hand and Logan dropped to the
ground like a stone. Magneto pulled the X-Man towards
him along the ground. Then he turned him over onto his
back.

Magneto smiled, ready to kill Logan. 'You never learn, do you?'

But before Magneto could do anything, Beast jumped through the fog behind him. The blue mutant pushed four cure darts into Magneto.

Magneto looked at the darts in disbelief and fell to his knees. 'I'm . . .' he began.

'One of them,' Logan finished.

Jean Grey watched cold and unfeeling as Magneto's body shook with pain.

'This is what they want for all of us,' Magneto shouted to Jean as he became human. But she wasn't really Jean now – she was the Phoenix. Her skin was grey and her eyes were black and angry.

'It's over, Jean,' Logan cried. 'It's over.'

But at that moment government soldiers finally arrived over the bridge. They had guns full of the cure and they fired hundreds of darts into the air. Immediately the Phoenix made a barrier with her mind. It was like a huge glass wall and the darts fell useless to the ground. Then she rose into the air, her long red hair waving around her. She looked at the soldiers and . . .

'No!' Logan shouted, but nothing could stop her now. In a second the soldiers and their guns exploded into pieces. Her power was out of control. It came from her in great waves. Pieces of metal flew through the air, fires started, and the sea rose up around the island. Her power was going to kill everybody, destroy everything . . .

Beast shouted, 'Get everybody off the island!'

People began to run, humans and mutants. Bobby saw Kitty with Leech and he helped them to leave the island. Storm wanted Logan to leave, too. But Logan called out, 'I'm the only one who can stop her!'

He started to walk towards the Phoenix. He cried out to her, 'Jean!'

When she heard his cry, she shot a wave of power towards him, pushing him back. His skin shivered and little pieces of his clothes and skin flew from his body. But Logan's power was special – his body could heal itself immediately. He pushed against her power and took another painful step towards her. Then another and another.

The light around the Phoenix was burning brighter and brighter. Logan had never known pain like this, but he did not stop – he loved Jean too much. At last he reached her.

She looked at the people escaping. 'You would die for them?' she asked but her voice didn't sound human.

'Not for them,' answered Logan. 'For you, Jean.'

For a moment the Phoenix was gone and Jean's beautiful face returned. 'Save me!' she cried. Logan moved closer, 'I love you,' he said. They were going to kiss . . . but then, he pushed his claws right through the Phoenix.

In her final seconds, Jean looked into Logan's eyes. She gave him one last grateful smile, and then died in his arms. Now it was all over.

Back at the school in Westchester they made a grave for Jean next to the graves of Scott and the Professor. The graves were in the school gardens – a calm and beautiful place for Jean to rest at last.

Some time after the X-Men had returned to the school, Bobby was walking to his room. He opened the door and saw his girlfriend sitting on the bed.

'Rogue! You're back,' he said in surprise.

She got up and moved closer to him. 'I'm sorry, Bobby. I had to.'

'This isn't what I wanted,' Bobby said quietly. He knew what she had done.

Rogue smiled. 'I know. It's what *I* want.'

She held out her hand and Bobby could see that she wasn't wearing gloves. For the first time, he held her hand in his. She had chosen to take the cure and at last they could be together.

In a park just outside San Francisco, an old man sat alone. He sat and just looked at the metal chess pieces in front of him. He remembered the games that he played long ago with his 'old friend', Charles Xavier. Back then he was Magneto, one of the most powerful mutants in the world. Now he was nothing.

He looked and looked at the chess pieces on the table in front of him. Then he lifted his right hand and, very slowly, one of the pieces started to move . . .

THE FILM

X-Men: The Last Stand, the third X-Men movie, first came out in cinemas in May 2006. It made over $123 million in its first weekend in the USA! Then it went on to make over $455 million in cinemas around the world.

Brett Ratner with Patrick Stewart (Professor Xavier)

THE DIRECTOR

The director of the first two X-Men films, Bryan Singer, wasn't able to work on *X-Men: The Last Stand*. Brett Ratner was chosen as the new director. He wanted the film to be really exciting. And he wanted to keep the style and feel of the first two films.

OLD FACES

Most of the characters from the first two X-Men films are in the third movie. But in *X-Men: The Last Stand* we see some of them in a new light:

● *Cyclops* cannot accept the death of his girlfriend, Jean Grey, at Alkali Lake. He is no longer the strong leader he was before.

● *Storm* becomes a stronger leader in this film. She speaks out against the cure for mutants. She decides Xavier's school must continue after his death. And, at the end of the film, she takes Xavier's place as head of the school.

● *Logan* had never been certain he wanted to be a part of the X-Men. In this film, in the final scenes, he becomes the leader of the team.

● *Jean Grey* returns and shows the darker, more powerful side of her personality – the part known as the Phoenix.

NEW FACES

In *The Last Stand* we see lots of mutants who weren't in the first two films. Here are just a few…

● *Beast* was one of Xavier's first X-Men. He is a politician and works for mutant rights. He also fights with the X-Men in the war against Magneto. He is very quick, strong and intelligent.

● *Juggernaut* is a fighting machine. His body is huge and he is amazingly strong – it can break straight though walls. Also when he starts to run, nothing can stop him! He joins Magneto when Magneto frees him from the prison truck.

● *Callisto* joins Magneto after the meeting at the church against the cure. She has super-speed and can 'feel' the powers of other mutants. She can also find mutants anywhere in the world.

● *Quill* joins Magneto at the same time as Callisto and Arclight. He has the power to shoot long black needles from his body. These needles are very dangerous as Dr Rao discovers near the end of the film.

● *Arclight* can make sound waves that can destroy anything she chooses. Like Quill and Callisto she has tattoos on her body to show she is proud to be a mutant.

> **Have you seen any of the X-Men films? Which one did you like best? Why? Which character do you like best? Why?**

AMAZING ACTION

One of the film's most amazing moments happens when Magneto lifts the Golden Gate Bridge and flies it across the water to Alcatraz. To film this, they built a full-size model of part of the bridge. The film-makers used computers to show the rest of the bridge.

Many of the action scenes used real actors. When Colossus throws Logan, the actor, Hugh Jackman, was pulled through the air on a wire. He reached a speed of 129 kilometres an hour!

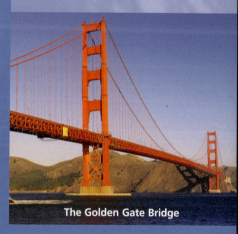

The Golden Gate Bridge

> **What do these words mean? You can use a dictionary.**
> **character   model   tattoo**
> **scene   wire**

MARVEL AND THE X-MEN COMICS

Professor Charles Xavier and his team of X-Men were around a long time before the X-Men films. They first appeared in a Marvel comic in 1963. What do you know about Marvel and the X-Men comics?

MARVEL COMICS

The company started in 1939 but it didn't use the name Marvel Comics until later. One of its first super-heroes was Captain America, a character who is still popular today. By 1961 the company was using the name Marvel Comics. Around this time there was an explosion of new super-hero comics. A young writer called Stan Lee joined artist Jack Kirby to make a comic called the *Fantastic Four*. More Marvel characters followed, including Spider-Man and the Hulk. In 1963, Stan Lee and Jack Kirby introduced the X-Men.

THE FIRST X-MEN

At first Stan Lee wanted to call the comic 'The Mutants', but he thought that readers might not understand this name. Readers might also expect his teenage characters to be happy and confident because of their special powers. But really these young super-heroes had many problems, hopes and fears. And because most humans hated mutants and were afraid of them, these teenage mutants often felt very frightened and alone.

All of the first team of the X-Men are in *The Last Stand* – Jean Grey (in the comics she is called Marvel Girl), Cyclops, Iceman, Beast, and Angel (Warren Worthington Junior in the film). Their characters and their stories are quite different from in the comics.

The cover of a Fantastic Four comic

DID YOU KNOW ...?

Stan Lee appears in many of the films of his comics. You can see him in the first scene of the film *X-Men: The Last Stand*. When Charles Xavier and Eric Lensherr visit Jean's house, Lee is a neighbour watering his garden.

THE NEW X-MEN

During the 1960s, the X-Men comics weren't as successful as some other Marvel comics. By the end of 1960s the company stopped making new stories about the team. But the comic was brought back to life in 1975.

The new X-Men were very different. Some of the old faces were there – including Cyclops and Jean Grey – but there were new characters like Logan and Storm. The new *X-Men* became the most popular comic in the world, with several different comics about the mutants.

The cover of an X-Men comic

FROM COMIC TO FILM

Some of the ideas for *X-Men: The Last Stand* came from two famous stories in the comics:

● In a 1980 story, Jean Grey seems to die and then comes back with much more power. She is called the Phoenix, but the reason for her return and new powers is very different from in the film.

● In 2004, there was a story in the comic called 'Gifted'. In this story, Dr Kavita Rao discovers a 'cure' for mutants.

But the film changes many other things from the X-Men comic. For example, in the comic . . .

● Leech is a small green boy.

● Juggernaut isn't a mutant. He is Charles Xavier's step-brother.

● Callisto cannot sense other mutants' powers.

> Have you read any Marvel comics?
> Which ones? Who are your favourite
> super-heroes? Why?

> What do these words mean?
> You can use a dictionary.
> super-hero   scene
> step-brother   sense

SAN FRANCISCO

Much of the action in *X-Men: The Last Stand* happens in San Francisco, a beautiful city on the west coast of the United States. Some of the most exciting scenes in the film happen at two famous sights near San Francisco – the Golden Gate Bridge and the island of Alcatraz.

THE GOLDEN GATE BRIDGE

One of the most famous bridges in the world, the Golden Gate Bridge joins the city of San Francisco with the area to the north.

HOW LONG DID IT TAKE TO BUILD THE BRIDGE?

Four years. Eleven men died during the work. The bridge opened in 1937.

HOW SAFE IS THE BRIDGE?

The area around San Francisco has had many earthquakes. The bridge is designed to move up to 8 metres from side to side during an earthquake.

WHY ISN'T THE BRIDGE GOLDEN?

The bridge's name isn't because of its colour. In the 1840s, an army officer thought that the land in this part of California looked like part of Istanbul called the Golden Horn. Soon the area was known as the 'Golden Gate'.

HOW MANY PEOPLE CROSS THE BRIDGE?

Lots! Over 40 million cars cross the bridge each year. Around 9 million tourists come to see the bridge every year.

> Have you been to the USA?
> What famous sights did you see?
> If not, what famous sights would you like to see?

THE NUMBERS ...

- 1966 metres long
- 27 metres wide
- Weight: 100,000 tonnes
- Highest point: 44 metres above the sea
- Lowest point: 30 metres below the sea

ALCATRAZ

Alcatraz is a rocky island in the middle of San Francisco Bay.

WHY IS ALCATRAZ FAMOUS?

The government built a prison on the island. Until 1963 the prison was home to some of the USA's most dangerous criminals. It was given the name 'The Rock'.

WERE THERE ANY FAMOUS PRISONERS?

Al Capone was probably the most famous prisoner. He was a gangster who ruled Chicago's criminal underworld in the 1920s.

Al Capone

Robert Stroud, a famous murderer, became even more famous when his story was made into a film, *The Birdman of Alcatraz*.

WHAT HAPPENED AFTER ...?

In 1969 a Native American group moved onto Alcatraz. They said that the island belonged to them. They lived there until 1971. Now the island is an important tourist sight in San Francisco. Tourists can take a boat to the island and visit the old prison buildings.

> **What do these words mean?**
> **You can use a dictionary.**
> earthquake   army   bay   gangster
> Native American   raft

ESCAPING 'THE ROCK'

Many prisoners tried to escape from 'The Rock'. Prison records say that nobody successfully escaped, but some people think that this isn't true. The Anglin brothers and Frank Morris tried to escape on a raft made out of fifty coats! The prison said that the men died during the escape, but the bodies were never found. Also, the Anglin brothers' family said that they received postcards from South America!

Prisoners on Alcatraz

PROLOGUE – CHAPTER 3

Before you read

You can use a dictionary for this section.

1 Use these words to answer the questions.

beam   needle   lightning   fog   claw   laboratory   cure   cell

Which …

a) is part of a cat's foot?

b) is like thick cloud?

c) can hit trees / buildings during a storm?

d) is a small room for a prisoner?

e) is a place where scientists work?

f) is long and very sharp?

g) is long and light?

h) can make a sick person better?

2 Use these words to complete the sentences.

announce   control   hug   heal   mind   humans   power   exploded

a) He tried to … the plane but it crashed to the ground.

b) Her leg took a long time to … after the accident.

c) All mutants have a special … .

d) My sister and I always … when we say hello.

e) He was a great scientist with a brilliant … .

f) The enemy's plane … when our guns hit it.

g) Most … are afraid of mutants.

h) They will … the news on TV tonight.

After you read

3 Complete the sentences with these names.

Mystique   Scott   Hank McCoy   Xavier

a) … visited Jean Grey when she was a teenager.

b) … can't stop thinking about Jean Grey.

c) … was caught and put in a cell.

d) … tells the X-Men about the mutant 'cure'?

CHAPTERS 4-6

Before you read

4 Match the two columns. You can use a dictionary.

a)	barrier	i)	dead
b)	conscious	ii)	stop
c)	dart	iii)	tie
d)	grave	iv)	cold
e)	shiver	v)	shoot
f)	strap	vi)	mind

5 Guess the answers to these questions.

a) What or who will Scott find at Alkali Lake?

b) Will Mystique escape from prison?

c) Who will die in these chapters?

d) Who will leave the school to take the 'cure'?

Now read chapters 4–6. Were your guesses right?

After you read

6 Put these events in order.

a) Storm and Logan find Jean's body on the beach.

b) Mystique becomes human.

c) Scott finds Jean alive.

d) Xavier explains about Jean's other personality.

e) Jean asks Logan to kill her.

f) Warren Worthington Junior flies away.

7 Answer the questions.

a) Where does Xavier find Jean?

b) Why do Storm and Logan cry tears of disbelief?

c) Why does Rogue leave the school?

8 What do you think?

a) Were you surprised that Magneto left Mystique? Why or why not?

b) What will Magneto do now he has Jean Grey?

CHAPTERS 7–10

Before you read

9 Which is which? You can use a dictionary.

camp   chess   soldier

a) There are thirty-two pieces in this game.
b) He or she usually has a gun.
c) You usually see tents in this place.

10 Answer these questions.

a) Chapter 7 is 'War Begins'. Who is this war between?
b) Chapter 8 is 'X-Men Together'. Which six X-Men go to fight?
c) Chapter 10 is 'Logan's Choice'. What choice must Logan make?

Now read chapters 7–10. Were your answers right?

After you read

11 True or false? Correct the false sentences.

a) Storm sends Worthington Junior away.
b) Logan hears Scott's voice in his head.
c) The President sends soldiers to protect the Worthington buildings.
d) Magneto moves Alcatraz to the Golden Gate Bridge.
e) Juggernaut reaches Leech before Kitty.
f) Bobby Drake beats his old friend Pyro.

12 What happens to these people?

a) Dr Rao
b) Warren Worthington Senior
c) Leech
d) Magneto
e) Jean Grey

13 What do you think?

a) In the end, who was stronger, Jean or the 'Phoenix'?
b) Rogue took the cure. Did she do the right thing?
c) What is going to happen to Magneto? Will his power return?